Circle Tim

a resource book for Infant, Junior and Secondary Schools

Teresa

With thanks to:

Our colleagues in Glou   993

Miss Lavis, staff and   eir

Embl

Meg

Wendy Solon

In memory

Circle Time is used widely in schools because teachers and young people love it. Nobody told us to do it - the word spread and amongst those who carried the word was a remarkable bookseller called Madeleine Lindley. She promoted Circle Time with enthusiasm - teachers responded by finding a place in the curriculum for Circle Time. Thank you.

Lucky Duck is more than a publishing house and training agency. George Robinson and Barbara Maines founded the company in the 1980's when they worked together as a head and psychologist developing innovative strategies to support challenging students.

They have an international reputation for their work on bullying, self-esteem, emotional literacy and many other subjects of interest to the world of education.

George and Barbara have set up a regular news-spot on the website. Twice yearly these items will be printed as a newsletter. If you would like to go on the mailing list to receive this then please contact us:

Lucky Duck Publishing Ltd. 3 Thorndale Mews, Clifton, Bristol, BS8 2HX, UK

Phone: 0044 (0)117 973 2881
Fax: 044 (0)117 973 1707

e-mail newsletter@luckyduck.co.uk
website www.luckyduck.co.uk

ISBN 1 873 942 55 9

Published by Lucky Duck Publishing Ltd
3 Thorndale Mews, Clifton, Bristol
BS8 2HX, UK

www.luckyduck.co.uk

Commissioned and Edited by George Robinson
Designed by Barbara Maines
Printed in the UK by Antony Rowe Ltd, Chippenham, Wiltshire

CONTENTS

FOREWORD

The National Curriculum has seemed to many teachers to be a straight-jacket that takes away the flexibility to pursue issues that arise in everyday events in the classroom. Whilst "Circle Time" has an obvious part to play in the curriculum as an opportunity to develop speaking and listening, it should be seen as fulfilling an essential role in the Spiritual and Moral development of young people.

Schools should be aware that Circle Time can provide a forum for discussion of important issues; relationships, equal rights, friendship, freedom, justice, and is therefore an essential part of the National Curriculum.

In the N.C. Council's discussion paper on Spiritual and Moral Development, (1993) they state,

> "It has to do with relationships with other people.... It has to do with the universal search for individual identity, with our response to challenging experiences.... It is to do with the search for meaning and purpose in life."
> (page 2.)

Circle Time provides a vehicle by which children as individual members of a group can explore their experiences and individuality, balanced against the experiences and views of others.

The discussion document clearly states that "self-knowledge, relationships, feelings and emotions are an essential part of the spiritual and moral development of young people.

> Self Knowledge. An awareness of oneself in terms of thoughts, feelings, emotions, responsibilities and experiences; a growing understanding and acceptance of individual identity; the development of self-respect.
> Relationships. Recognising and valuing the worth of each individual; developing a sense of community; the ability to build up relationships with others.
> Feelings and Emotions. The sense of being moved by beauty or kindness; hurt by injustice or aggression; a growing awareness of when it is important to control emotions and feelings, and how to learn to use such feelings as a source of growth."
> (page 3)

The document emphasises the importance of the strengths of Circle Time. Without the opportunity of learning cooperation children would be, "deprived of self-understanding and, potentially of the ability to understand others, they may experience difficulty in co-existing with neighbours and colleagues to the detriment of their social development."
(page 3)

Though the document does not advocate a model of linear progression it does specify the steps by which spiritual development might be achieved. Circle Time provides the methods and process by which these steps can be achieved:

"recognising the existence of others as independent from oneself."
"becoming aware of and reflecting on experience."
"questioning and exploring the meaning of experience."
"understanding and evaluating a range of possible responses and interpretations."
"developing personal views and insights."
"applying the insights gained with increasing degrees of perception to one's own life."
(page 3.)

Circle Time encourages spiritual and moral development by providing opportunities to:
"- discuss matters of personal concern;
- develop relationships with adults and peers;
- develop a sense of belonging to a community;
- experience silence and reflection;"
(page 7.)

Though teachers should not need a justification for providing the opportunity for children to think and talk about themselves and others, Circle Time can be justified in enhancing speaking and listening skills and also in providing the opportunity for young people to explore aspects of self and others in terms of spiritual and moral development."

"From 1993 OFSTED will be inspecting and evaluating schools' provision for spiritual and moral development.... Evidence of such provision will be gathered through:
- observation of lessons and other aspects of the school's work...
- whether the school..... offers opportunities in the curriculum for reflective and aesthetic experience and the discussion of questions about meaning and purpose."
(page 9.)

The inclusion of Circle Time in the school curriculum provides a framework for this work to take place. The various activities in this book provide the structure, confidence and skills to build awareness of self and others. The process of Circle Time supports an ethos within which the adults can guide the spiritual and moral development of the pupils.

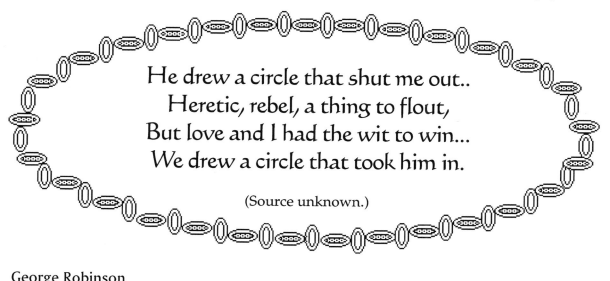

He drew a circle that shut me out..
Heretic, rebel, a thing to flout,
But love and I had the wit to win...
We drew a circle that took him in.

(Source unknown.)

George Robinson
August 1993

CIRCLE TIME

Circle Time brings together teacher and children in an enjoyable atmosphere of co-operation. It is a time set aside each week when children and their teacher sit in a circle and take part in games and activities designed to increase self awareness, awareness of others, self esteem, co-operation, trust and listening skills. The activity helps everyone to understand what is important to them and their friends. Children become more able to express their feelings and it encourages greater tolerance between girls and boys. As children learn more about themselves and each other a warm and supportive group atmosphere is built, along with improved relationships.

Self Esteem

For teachers the issue of a child's self esteem is a vitally important consideration. Self esteem affects a child's behaviour in all aspects of school life including academic and social. Research has shown strong links between positive self esteem and success at school Purkey, W. (1970), Lawrence, D. (1973 and 1988) and Burns, R. B. (1982). Children with a positive high self regard are more likely to achieve academically and less likely to be in trouble than children with poor or low self regard.

Below are listed some of the behaviour traits that might indicate low self regard:-

  - feeling uncomfortable with praise
  - unable to accept praise
  - unable to ask for needs to be met
  - critical and jealous of others
  - inability to be warm and affectionate
  - being negative about self and particularly in comparison with others
  - feeling unworthy and guilty
  - refusing to work in case of failure.

The games in Circle Time aim to break into those feelings, in a gentle and subtle way they encourage everyone to:-

  - praise themselves (I'm good at ....)
  - talk positively about self and achievements
  - be assertive about needs
  - give and accept compliments in a 'matter of fact' way
  - accept that things go wrong sometimes yet it does not fundamentally impinge on self worth
  - celebrate achievements and good times
  - be prepared to take risks, to have a go at unfamiliar work or activities.

National Curriculum

Circle Time meets the demands of the National Curriculum for English. Children are required to participate as speakers and listeners in whole class activities and to respond appropriately to simple and complex instructions given by both teacher and pupils and to convey accurately simple messages. You will find Circle Time activities fulfil all these requirements.

Listening and Speaking

When we introduced Circle Time to schools three years ago, teachers were exceptionally pleased with the impact it had on listening and speaking skills. Listening in particular is mentioned time and again. It also helps children to be patient and wait their turn. In the circle all children eventually have the opportunity to speak. They become better at waiting as they become more tolerant of others. The teacher is able to model acceptance and be non-judgmental.

Rules for the circle

We believe rules should be kept to a minimum, e.g. no more than one or two at a session. We usually only introduce the first rule, sometimes the first and the second rules are all that is required. However, we suggest you allow the rules to evolve as necessary. The same rule sometimes needs to be introduced time and again in different contexts with some classes and for particular individuals, but this is after all how we teach anything. Below is a list of rules we have needed from time to time, but we want to emphasise they may not all be needed.

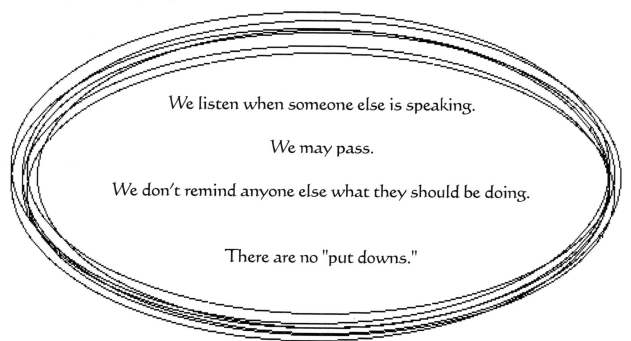

We listen when someone else is speaking.

We may pass.

We don't remind anyone else what they should be doing.

There are no "put downs."

The pass rule is best introduced as discretely as possible. You will find some children like to test the pass rule for one or two rounds. The novelty soon wears off.

Sometimes children are silly, for example, a child may say "I like to beat up my sister". It is best to ignore such a statement and move on in as neutral a way as possible. On the other hand it may be more appropriate to say dispassionately "I haven't given you much time to think, I'll come back to you". This gives the child the opportunity to redeem himself with a more acceptable statement. It is also a sharing of the responsibility. It is important to remember that everyone is equal within the circle and the interactions are not child-to-teacher but child to the circle.

Circle Ethos and Benefits.

The ethos of Circle Time is positive, encouraging and non-judgemental.

Children thoroughly enjoy Circle Time. They appreciate the opportunity to be listened to and to know that their turn will come. They enjoy hearing personal details about their teacher. They love being encouraged to feel that they are important and likeable individually and collectively.

The children one would least expect often plan and think through what their contribution will be. The articulation of their views and ideas improves along with the listening skills we have already mentioned. The circle can become a forum where class members are able to express their needs, negotiate and mediate. All this reduces the likelihood of problems and frustrations. Towards the end of the book there are suggestions on how Circle Time can help with friendship problems and open up the topic of bullying. Our experience tells us that teachers use it in creative and imaginative ways that are best for their unique situations.

Organisation of Circle Time.

It is best done in the classroom where you can keep the warm atmosphere you generate. The beginning or end of a session is the easiest time to rearrange chairs and desks. We would recommend that chairs are placed in a circle, leaving the centre free for movement within the circle. If the children are seated on the floor, as they get up and move around, the circle becomes distorted and the space they need to return to is lost. Opportunities for listening and eye-contact between all participants is a priority. We have found that the session runs much more smoothly if children are comfortable.

The activities should last for about twenty minutes to half an hour. Most younger children appreciate an ending activity.

The Games.

Most of the games listed are suitable for all ages. So many times infant teachers have commented to us how surprised they were by the level of articulation and understanding. Colleagues will know which games are suitable for their classes. Many of them are adaptable, for example the game "Finishing the Sentence" we use with infant and adult groups and all ages in between. Many of the games have variations on the theme, and we have listed the ones we know. We have called the Circle Time leader the facilitator because eventually it may be possible for the children to lead the sessions rather than the teacher.

Sources

Most of the games in this book are adaptations and variations devised by us over the last three years to suit the needs of the children and schools we have worked with.

Over the years we have used a great many sources. Some games have passed into common usage, others were given to us with the origin unknown. Many games are familiar to those in the Brownie-Guide and Cub-Scout movements.

For the purposes of this book we have listed in the reference section books we used frequently in the early stages. We would also like to particularly recommend the following as valuable additions to any staff room library.

100 Ways to Enhance Self Esteem in the Classroom - Canfield, J. and Wells, H. (1976) Prentice-Hall
Let's Co-operate - Mildred Masheder (1986) Peace Education.

Games, Games, Games - Woodcraft Folk.

Teresa Bliss and Jo Tetley - 1993.

To Summarise.

Circle Time encourages:-

 * cognitive skills such as ability to reflect, predict, question, concentrate, evaluate then recount in a concise manner,
 * interpersonal skills such as the ability to listen, explain feelings and motives, empathise, encourage others in a positive way and speak publicly,
 * it encourages a compassionate, sensitive and accepting attitude to others, developed in a spirit of generosity, openness and caring.

To do this:-

 * positive, simple rules are followed,
 * feelings are focused on,
 * awareness of self and others encouraged,
 * no judgements are made (by teachers or children),
 * personal responsibility is emphasised,
 * each member is valued,
 * everyone experiences sharing in a sensitive, positive yet fun way.

A Suggested Menu

Ideas below are for an initial session with infant, junior and secondary age children. For younger children talking about how we sit to listen (feet together, hands on laps) might be helpful. Start by talking about our Circle Time rule "We listen when someone else is speaking". Then enjoy the session with your class.

INFANTS

1   My Name. - page 16

(Facilitator starts, going around the circle from their left).

My name is ..... and so on around the circle.

2   Silent Statements (to change places). - page 23

Stand up and change places all children wearing something blue, laces on
their shoes, grey socks, wearing a cardigan, etc.

3   Finishing the Sentence. - page 29

(Facilitator starts going around the circle from their right).

My favourite colour is ....

(Go back to the child who couldn't say a colour, to encourage them to have
a turn).

4   Pass the Smile. - page 38

(Facilitator starts, going round circle from their left).

Make eye contact with person to your left and smile and so on around the
circle.

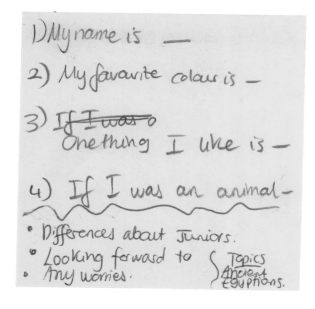

1) My name is ___

2) My favourite colour is ___

3) If I was o
   One thing I like is ___

4) If I was an animal ___

• Differences about Juniors.
• Looking forward to
• My worries.
  Topics
  Ancient
  Egyptians.

JUNIORS

1   My Name and the name of the person on my right. - page 16

2   Silent Statements. - page 23

Stand up and change places all those wearing:-

- buckles on their shoes; a "V" neck jumper; can swim a width of the pool; enjoy using the computer; watch (favourite "soap") on T.V., etc.

3   Finishing the Sentence. - page 29

My favourite animal is .... because ....

4   50 Ways of Moving. - page 33

5   Finishing the Sentence. - page 29

The thing I like doing best in school is...........

6   Pass the Squeeze. - page 38

SECONDARY

1 **Introduce self and person to left or right. - page 16**

2 **Silent Statements. - page 23**

Stand up and change places all those wearing black shoes; watched a favourite "soap" this week; walked to school.

3 **Finishing the Sentence. - page 29**

If I were a car I'd be .... because ....
If I were Prime Minister I'd .... because ....
I think all parents should ....
One thing that would make school better is if we ....

4 **The Magic Box. - page 37**

5 **Pass the Squeeze. - page 38**

PART 1

INTRODUCING GAMES

These games help children use their own names and names of classmates. They encourage a positive group feeling, help develop self esteem and awareness of peers.

MY NAME and Variations

Game 1   For the very young ones (3-5 years) the facilitator starts by saying "My name is ...." and encourages each child in the circle to say their name in turn around the circle using the whole sentence.

Game 2   The facilitator starts by saying "My name is Miss Jones". The first student to her right says "My name is John and this is Miss Jones". This process is continued around the circle until each person has said their name and introduced the person on their left.

Game 3   Say your name and introduce the people sitting either side.

Game 4   Each person introduces themselves and says how they feel "My name is Miss Jones and I'm feeling tired".

Game 5   Introduce yourself with an adjective that begins with the same letter as your name. E.g. "I am careful Colin".

Game 6   Introduce yourself with a verb, e.g. "I am Henry, hopping Henry".

Helpful hint:

Talking about and making lists of 'feeling words', adjectives and verbs (for games 4, 5 and 6) is a good idea before the game starts.

UP DOWN UP

This game looks very impressive watched from outside the circle.

Everyone sits in a circle and each time their name is called they stand up then sit down straight away.

The facilitator says the name of the person to their right, their own name, then the name of the person to the left.

The next person repeats the pattern.

BALL ROLLING

Materials needed: Soft ball.

Game 1   First person calls out the name of the person they have chosen and rolls the ball to them. That person then calls out the name of someone else and rolls the ball, and so on until everyone has had a turn.

Game 2   A child calls the name of the person she intends to roll the ball to and says something they like to do, e.g. "Emma, I like skipping", and rolls the ball to Emma.

Helpful hint:

Remind them to listen and remember who has had a turn so that each person's name is only called once.

NAME ASSOCIATION

A child is asked to talk about his name, e.g.

I like my name because ....

I don't like my name because ....

I would like my name to have been ....

Other people with my name in my family are ....

My parents chose my name because ....

NAME CHAIN

Each person moves once to the chair of the named person.

i.e. Jo calls Mary and moves to Mary's chair, Mary calls Peter and moves to Peter's chair.........

ACTION MIME

First person does one action, e.g. clap hands. Second person copies that mime and does one of their own, e.g. claps hands and clicks fingers. Third person copies the last action and adds one of their own, e.g. clicks fingers and smiles. Continue around circle, each child doing two actions each.

ALL CHANGE GAMES

Circle work

By Benyveis

These games are sometimes known as 'energisers'. They allow teachers to
move friendship groups or troublesome groups
in a subtle and fun way.

Helpful hint:-

It may be necessary if children are excitable, to remind them about moving
across the circle quietly and without touching anyone.

POSTMAN

Game 1 Facilitator gives everyone a number.

Facilitator calls out:

"The postman is calling at numbers two and twelve".

Children with these numbers change places.

If call is "collection time" all change places.

Game 2 Remove one chair from the circle. A child stands in the centre of the circle.

Facilitator calls out , "The postman is coming to (two numbers.) The child in the centre tries to reach a chair whilst the change-over takes place. (Only two goes in the centre allowed.)

FOLLOW ME

Game 1 Facilitator gives simple directions, e.g.

Take a step forward.

Touch toes.

Hands on head.

The class to follow directions.

Game 2 Simon says, giving quicker instructions.

TRAINS, BOATS & PLANES

NB: This is a good opportunity for the shy child to have the chance to instruct others. If it is played for too long the dominant ones hang back to be the last to sit down.

Game 1 Sit in a circle.

Each child is touched and told whether he is a train, boat or plane.

If the facilitator calls out "boats" the boats change places. If she calls out "transport" they all change places.

Facilitator removes one chair so that some one is left in middle. They call out what is to move. Suggest they only have one turn in the middle.

Game 2 Children are named crocodiles, elephants, and giraffes. Miming each animal, e.g. crocodiles extend arms and clap hands to show snapping mouths.

Facilitator calls out who is to move, children change places (most suitable for children 3-5 years).

Helpful hint:
When telling each child what they are going to be, e.g. train, boat or plane, make eye contact and put your hand on each shoulder - it helps them to remember.

MY EYES ARE ....

Game 1 Facilitator and children sit in a circle.

The facilitator calls out an eye colour.

All those with eyes that colour change seats.

Game 2 This game can be used as a way of pairing children, e.g. say all those with brown eyes stand up and come to the middle, now find a friend from the centre to sit next to.

Helpful hint:
More suitable for juniors and older children.

NEW FRIENDS

Place chairs in a circle. Children and teacher fill the floor space inside the circle.

All walk slowly round looking down. They are told not to look at or bump into anyone else.

Each person is touched on the shoulder by the facilitator and asked their name. They then sit down quietly.

Helpful hint: This is a good game for the beginning of term. It is also a game you can use with a new child being the facilitator.

SILENT STATEMENTS

We use this game every time, it is a way of making a statement about ourselves without speaking. It has many names, one of our favourites is "The Washing Line".

The facilitator makes a statement;

> All children wearing .... e.g. colours, clothes, etc.
> All children who can .... e.g. ride a bike, swim a width, etc.
> All children with ..... e.g. missing teeth, a brother, blue eyes, etc.
> All children who watch .... e.g. Neighbours, The Bill, etc.
> All children who will be ..... e.g. 10 next birthday, going on holiday etc.

All conforming stand up and change places with someone else also standing.

More Silent Statements suggested in this second edition : Change places if...

> You enjoy eating pizza, roast beef, cornflakes...
> You enjoy reading..
> You hate having a bath.
> You love watching football.
> You watch T.V. before school in the mornings.
> Your birthday is this term.
> You have never stayed away from home.
> You are concerned about the environment.
> Friends are very important to you
> You have a pet at home.
> Your eyes are blue / brown.
> You agree with school uniform.
> You would like to wear different clothes to school.
> To get to school you walk, cycle come by bus, car, train.

Helpful hint: For very young children (3-5 years) this can be broken down very simply.

Ask the children to look, very quietly, at the clothes they are wearing today e.g. "Look at our shoes and the colour they are and if they have laces or buckles". Then our socks, etc. and so on until we touch our hair "to see if we are wearing a ribbon or a hairband". Then put our hands on our laps.

> "Let's look at our shoes again".
>
> "If you have laces on your shoes please stand up".
>
> "Go to the middle of the circle".
>
> "Now find a different seat to sit in".

See also: Developing Circle Time.

GAMES TO ENCOURAGE SELF CONCEPT

These games help all children feel really good about themselves and because class-mates have contributed to each individual's good feeling, the whole class group has a positive, caring atmosphere.

I AM SPECIAL

Materials: A piece of A4 paper for each child, felt tip pens and masking tape.

Everyone in a circle.

Tape a piece of paper onto each child's back.

The children walk round the circle and write one positive comment on each sheet of paper with a felt tip pen.

When all the comments have been written the children sit back in a circle and read what has been written.

The children take turns to read out **one** statement that pleases them most.

IT'S MY DAY

Materials: One large sheet of paper and felt tip pens or marker pens.

Game 1   Teacher chooses one person to go out of room.

Each child takes turns to say something positive about that person.
"I like .... because ....

Teacher writes the name of the person who has gone out of the room on the paper and all the positive comments made by peers.

The child is called back in and each child reads out the statement he/she has made about classmate.

or   Teachers reads out the statement, while child listens.

The written sheet can be taken home.

This is a wonderful game for all ages.

Game 2   Each child has the opportunity to be 'special' once a term. On their special day they could wear a badge and have extra privileges and special jobs to do that they would find rewarding.

THIS IS ME

Aim: For children to make a positive statement about themselves.

Materials: An object that is nice to hold.

Children hold object, look at neighbour, turn body in chair and make a positive statement about themselves, e.g.

I like ....

I am good at ....

My favourite ....

Helpful hint:

This is a game to encourage making and maintaining appropriate eye contact with a friend. This is a very good game for infants or children with poor social skills. It is also a good game to use before you ask children to make statements about other children.

PARTNERS

Game 1 Group is paired off by numbers/fruits/letters or another fun way, e.g. elephant, mouse, elephant, mouse.

The children then turn their chairs to slightly face one another. They then share with a partner one or two things they enjoy doing, e.g. two television programmes they enjoy. Each child reports back what his partner enjoyed. This encourages listening.

Game 2 They can share two things they dislike doing or two foods they dislike eating.

Helpful hint:

This game is useful if you have established cliques and want to broaden friendship groups or wish to help a new child integrate.

SHARING GAMES

**These games enable children to express feelings that foster empathy,
a better understanding of one another,
greater co-operation and trust.**

INFORMATION SHARING

We suggest children are paired with someone they don't usually work/play with, or play a mixing up game first.

Game 1   Sit in a circle and work in pairs. Turn to face partner.

Remind them it is about listening to each other and reporting back to the circle.

Find two/three things they have in common, e.g. enjoy swimming, have a dog, favourite food.

When they are ready, turn to face circle, hands on laps.

Each takes it in turn to tell others what they have in common.

(Suggest to older children they do not include age, teacher and school but look for other things.)

Game 2   If anyone else in the circle also has in common what has been said, they should put up their hand. It is interesting to note how much we all have in common.

Game 3   In pairs person **A** tells the other as much as possible about himself, **B** listens carefully without speaking. After two minutes stop them. Person **B** then tells about himself while 'A' listens. After four minutes pairs face circle. Ask each person to introduce his partner, stating his name and something he has said about himself.

Check with each pair how it felt to be listened to without being interrupted.

Discuss listening skills, e.g. how we sit, body language and eye contact, etc.

Helpful hints:
Some pairs have to wait a while for their turn and find it hard to resist checking with their partners. Remind them it is important to listen to others and you will allow them to confer again when it is their turn if they need to.

See also: Developing Circle Time.

FINISHING THE SENTENCE

The facilitator always starts and the sentence is taken up by each person in the circle. Choose from....

My favourite colour is ....
My favourite animal is ....
If I was an animal I would be .... because ....
If I were Prime Minister I'd ....
The nicest thing I ever did for anyone ....
The nicest thing anyone ever did for me ....
The nicest thing I ever did for myself ....
I would love to......................
If I were a magician I would ....
I feel happy when ....
When I am older ....
If I were a parent I would ....
I think all children should ....
If I wasn't here I'd like to be ....
If I were a car I'd be ....
Sometimes I pretend I am ....
The best day I ever had ....
The worst day I ever had ....
My hero at the moment is .... because ....
If I was a piece of furniture I would be ....
If I was a colour I would be ....
A time I was really scared was when............
One thing that would make this class better is if we ....
One person I'd like to spend the day with is ....
It makes me angry when ....
One thing that's good about this class is ....

Pretend you have just won a great deal of money, think of someone you would give it away to:-

I would give it to .... because ....
I would spend it on .... because ....
I wouldn't spend it on .... because ....

Helpful hint:

> If the child is not ready to complete the sentence they can say "pass" and you can return to them when you have finished the round. Encourage all children to take part. Choose statements that are suitable for the age and needs of the class.

Some additional unfinished sentences suggested in the second edition.

Cooperation is needed because ....

Something I enjoy doing is ....

When I am older I would like to be / do ....

Something I would like to achieve this year is ....

The achievement I am most proud of is ....

A friend is someone who ....

If I had the courage I would ....

If I were a teacher I would......................

.... is a person in this class / school I would like to know better.

The thing I enjoy doing most at school is ....

The thing I enjoy doing most at home is ....

It makes me feel good when ....

I value people who ....

All schools should teach ....

One sport I would love to try is ....

I would love to go to .... on holiday because ....

My favourite book is .... because ....

My favourite possession at home is .... because ....

The thing that most concerns me at school is ....

The thing that concerns me most in the world is ....

The quality I look for in a friend is .... because ....

I am a .... sort of person

Two words that best describe me are .... and ....

My favourite food is ....

Three possessions I would take to a desert island are ...., ...

I am happiest with my family when ....

I am happiest with my friends when ....

I would like to teach everyone in the world ....

One of the best things about my parents is ....

One thing I would like people to remember me for is ....

One thing I would like people to say about me is ....

The thing I admire most about my mother / father is ....

.... is something I do well.

.... is something I am getting better at.

Note

> When an activity mentions terms like "parents", "mother" or "father" it is helpful to teach the group to substitute the name or term used to identify an alternative carer if appropriate.

WISHING WELL

You have just freed a genie from a bottle and you have got three wishes, one for yourself, one for your family and one for the whole world.

> "For me I wish.....
> "For my family I wish....
> "For the world I wish....

GUESS WHO

Game 1   The facilitator starts by saying three things about someone in the circle, e.g. it's a boy, his name begins with "C", and he is good at making things.

When the three things have been said, any child who guesses the identity of the child described can raise a hand. If the guess is correct this child can then take a turn to describe another child.

Invite the children in the circle (especially the quiet ones) to have a go.

Remind them to try not to make it too obvious by staring at the person they are describing.

Game 2   The children and the facilitator write out some biographical information that describes them but does not make it too obvious who they are, e.g. include a description of the sort of person they think they are, hobbies, unusual things about their family. (Put their name on top corner). When each person has done this collect cards/pieces of paper into envelope or box. Each Circle Time session pick out three or four cards to read out for them to guess.

LISTEN, CO-OPERATE
& HAVE FUN

Circle for Harmony

Circle Time is what brings Life together, if you
don't do it then you are the Loser.
So, Circle for harmony.
It's the only way if your sad or woried
this is the way to end your sadnes.
So circle for harmony.

**These games help develop listening skills, co-operation,
concentration and imagination.
They are also fun.**

50 WAYS OF MOVING

Game 1   Sit in a circle, with one extra chair or facilitator stands leaving a chair vacant.

Facilitator calls one person to start moving from his chair to the empty chair in any way he chooses, e.g. hopping, jumping, or like an animal.

Another child across the circle from the empty chair is then chosen to move, trying not to copy the other person.

All children, including the facilitator, have a turn at moving in different ways to the empty chair.

Game 2   Two children at a time could be chosen to move to empty chairs.

It may be helpful to establish a rule, e.g. no running.

Helpful hint:

For younger children this is a good game to follow on from "Finishing the Sentence" e.g. My favourite animal, you can then suggest they move like their animal.

FOLLOW THE LEADER

Facilitator starts by saying "watch me and do as I do". Then put hands on lap, hands in the air, cross a leg, etc. giving children an idea of the sort of moves to make. The children copy. Suggest that they make their observations with a quick glance and avoid staring at the leader.

Explain the game. One person is chosen to go out of the room. Then one person is chosen to initiate the actions, e.g. hands on head, clapping, etc. Everyone copies the actions as though in unison so it is hard to guess the leader. This may take some practice.

The first person returns, stands in the centre of the circle and has two guesses at who is leading the actions. The facilitator then chooses two more people, one to go out and one to lead.

GUARDING THE KEYS

Explain that this game is all about being good listeners.

They are going to be listening for a **positive sound of key jangling** (demonstrate by jangling keys), **not** the sounds of footsteps or anyone moving.

Make up a story about the keys, how important they are, what they are for, etc.

Ask them to help you to guard these keys because someone in the circle is going to try and take them away.

Explain the game:-

A bunch of keys is placed in the centre of the circle.

All close eyes, with no peeping. The facilitator keeps his/her eyes open to check no one peeps.

The facilitator taps a child on the shoulder, they open their eyes, that child then tries to pick up the keys without being heard.

When they can hear the sound of the keys being moved, without opening their eyes, children in the circle point to where the sound is coming from.

If pointed at directly, the child in the middle stops where s/he is.

They all open their eyes. Those pointing to the noise are "accurate listeners".

Child replaces keys in the middle and returns to seat.

The Facilitator then chooses another child to pick up the keys.

EXPRESSIONS

Game 1   The facilitator is the first person to make a face to the person on his left, this expression is copied. That person then turns to the person on his left and makes a face of his own.

The game is continued until all in the circle have copied a face and made one of their own.

Game 2   A variation of this can be to copy the emotion; that is the facilitator makes a face, the emotion has to be guessed. The child then makes a face indicating a different emotion and the next child in the circle has to guess the emotion.

Objective is to help children recognise how their feelings are reflected in their facial expression and that a happy face not only makes them feel better but will also influence other people.

This can be extended by speculation on what might have caused the emotion, however this can be lengthy.

LISTEN AND TOUCH

For younger children.

Facilitator calls:

"Everyone touch .... (a colour, person or object) **with** .... (your thumb, little finger, elbow etc.)"

Concepts such as left/right can be introduced into this game.

THUNDER

Game 1   The facilitator leads the thunderstorm.

Each child must follow the person on their left. (Ensure the child knows who is to their left).

The facilitator starts by rubbing their hands together saying "this is the sound of leaves rustling in the wind". The person on his/her right then copies and it is repeated around the circle.

The facilitator then changes to tapping two fingers saying "gentle rain begins to fall".

Next the facilitator changes to clapping saying "the rain is getting harder and louder" as clapping goes round the circle.

The hand clapping changes to thigh slapping, then stamping feet until all are doing the same action saying "rain is pouring, thunder is rolling."

The circle then reverses the actions, e.g. feet stop, thigh slapping goes to hand clapping, to two finger tapping, to rustling leaves noise, then silence. Hands in lap.

The storm has ceased.

Game 2   Infants can play this game but they all have to follow the facilitator instead of one another. Teachers can make a more elaborate story and invent new sounds.

THE WAVE

This co-operative game is great fun and very impressive from the outside.

Everyone sits on the floor in a circle, leaning forward, with hands flat on the floor.

Facilitators hands go up in the air then immediately back down to the floor. Next person copies the action of the facilitator, and so on in quick succession.

MAGIC BOX (a mime game.)

Facilitator places an imaginary box into the middle of the circle and lifts the lid.

S/he silently demonstrates an object taken from the box, e.g. a baby, a football, a banana.

Children then raise their hands when they guess the object.

The child who guesses correctly takes something from the magic box and mimes it.

LET'S LAUGH

Aim: This game involves trying to get someone to laugh (without touching).

One person stands in centre of circle with the intention of not laughing.

People in circle take turns to ask the person in the middle questions, e.g. "What do you brush your teeth with?"

Person in the centre always answers with "Sausages or "Pink frogs", or something else that is silly.

If person in the centre laughs then s/he must change places with someone else, and so on.

Helpful hint:
Limit number of tries at making someone laugh to three, otherwise the game can take too long for some players.

FINISHING GAMES

Game 1   *Pass the Smile.*

Facilitator turns to person on their right, makes eye contact and smiles, that person turns to person on their right and smiles, until everyone in the circle has had a turn.

Game 2   *Pass the Squeeze.*

(Decide whether it will begin from the facilitator's left or right side).

Everyone in the circle joins hands.

Facilitator starts by gently squeezing the hand of the person next to them, then the squeeze is passed around the circle as quickly as possible without a sound (like an electric current)

Helpful hint:
Keep joined hands in view so that the squeeze can be watched as it goes around.

PART 2

The Development of Circle Time

DEVELOPING CIRCLE TIME

Circle Time will give class groups practice at being assertive instead of aggressive and experience feelings of respect and acceptance from one another. It will help them have a more receptive and caring attitude to each other. It will also encourage increased personal responsibility for behaviour.

It is at this point that the teacher will be able to move the class into becoming a group that is ready to be more autonomous and make decisions for themselves. Problems and concerns can be brought to the group for discussion and resolution.

If Circle Time is used regularly and children are encouraged by the teacher to work non-judgementally and to listen with respect to one another, considerable trust as well as co-operation within the class group will develop over a period of time. Children's articulation of feelings and needs will have helped awareness of themselves and their peers.

Themes

Below are some ideas for developing the work that takes place during Circle Time. There may be particular problems or issues that need to be dealt with for the class. We give examples of how the games can be used to deal with some very serious issues. It needs to be explained that a theme will be taken for the session. It is best that the teacher should be the facilitator in the first instance.

Stealing

This is a problem that crops up in all schools from time to time. You may or may not know who is responsible but you can begin to deal with the **feelings** it generates within the group and how the thief and victim may feel. It is important to avoid inadvertent name calling or labelling, for example, a sentence completion beginning; "a thief is ....", "a victim is ...", is **labelling** and should not be used.

It is as damaging to label the victim as it is to label the thief. It is always more productive to work on **feelings**.

It is safer to start working without words, so silent statements such as ....

"Change places ......

     ..... if you are aware stealing has happened;
     ...... if stealing worries you;
     ...... if stealing does not worry you;
     ...... if you or a friend have had anything stolen", etc.

Never ask for public confessions.

Next you can move onto **"Finishing Sentences"**, for example ....

> "I think a thief may feel ....",
> "I think it would feel .... to have something stolen",
> "I feel .... knowing stealing is happening".

Below are some ideas for more themes.

Relationships in Class

The friendship groups are of great significance to children. The teaching and curriculum can be of the highest quality but if children are anxious or worried about broken friendships then it can pass them by. A great deal of valuable learning time can be wasted by children upset by classroom relationships. Below are some examples of how you can use silent statements and finishing sentences in the way suggested above.

Silent statements.

"Change places if ....

> .... your friends are important to you",
> .... you have friends in other classes in the school",
> .... you believe you are a good friend".

Finishing sentences.

> A friend is ....
> A friend shows s/he cares by ....
> A friend would never ....
> When I am unhappy my friend ....
> When I am happy my friend ....

Arguing/Fighting

Again another issue that arises frequently with young people.

Mostly they sort out problems among themselves, however very often after such problems have been sorted out there has been a winner and a loser. In such scenarios usually there are residual feelings of anger, resentment, guilt or disappointment. To deal with this you could start with **silent statements** and **finishing sentences** that focus on feelings.

You could start with **silent statements** such as;

Change places if ....

.... you feel angry when you don't get your own way,

.... you feel upset at being called names,

.... you have seen two people fighting/arguing in this class.

Finishing sentences.........

I feel .... when I fall out with a friend,

I feel .... when I think a friend has been unkind,

I feel .... when I see two members of the class arguing.

I feel .... when I hear someone called names.

I feel .... when I am called names.

Other Themes

There are many themes you can explore, for example:-

new experiences,   *rules at home,*
changing schools,   *anger,*
relationships with parents,   *sibling rivalry,*
relationships with teachers,   *homework,*
rules at school,   *bullying.*

Bullying needs extreme caution and care in handling. There is an excellent video and accompanying workbook by Maines and Robinson (1992) suggested in the reference section.

Before you take a theme with the class make a careful plan setting out the sentences you will use to develop the theme and the non-verbal responses you will ask of the group.

Suggestion Box

You can provide a box for the young people to add their own ideas and themes.

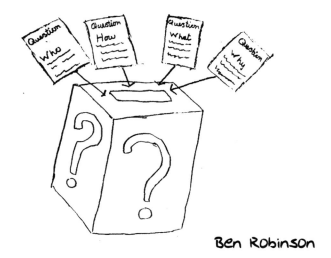

Ben Robinson

42

REFERENCES and FURTHER READING

Burns, D. (1982) - Self Concept Development and Education - Holt Rinehart and Winston, Sydney.

Canfield, J. and Wells, H. (1976) - 100 Ways to Enhance Self Concept in the Classroom - Prentice-Hall, Englewood Cliffs, New Jersey.

C.A.S.E. (1999). Six years of Circle Time. Lucky Duck Publishing Ltd.

Co-operation in the Classroom - a project pack for teachers. Global Co-operation for a better World. 98, Tennyson Road, London NW6 7SB

Games, Games, Games. - produced by The Woodcraft Folk.

Lawrence, D. (1973) - Improved Reading through Counselling Work - Ward Lock, London.

Lawrence, D. (1988) - Enhancing Self Esteem in the Classroom - Paul Chapman Publishing Ltd.

Masheder, M. (1986) - Let's Co-operate. Peace Education.

Masheder, M. (1989) - Let's Play Together. Green Print - The Merlin Press Ltd., London.

Maines, B. and Robinson, G. (1992). Michael's being Bullied, The No Blame Approach. Lucky Duck Publishing Ltd.

National Curriculum Council. (1993). Spiritual and Moral Development; a discussion paper.

Purkey, W. (1970) - Self Concept and School Achievement. - Prentice-Hall, Englewood Cliffs, New Jersey.

Robinson, G. and Maines, B., (1988) - A Bag of Tricks, the video and handbook. Lucky Duck Publishing Ltd.

Robinson, G. and Maines, B., (1999) - Circle Time Resources. Lucky Duck Publishing Ltd.

Ways and means; an approach to problem solving.. The Handbook of Kingston Friends Workshop Group.

White, M. (1999) Magic Circles. Lucky Duck Publishing Ltd.

White, M. (1999) Picture This. Lucky Duck Publishing Ltd.

Notes

Don't forget to visit our website for all our latest publications, news and reviews.

www.luckyduck.co.uk

New publications every year on our specialist topics:

- **Emotional Literacy**
- **Self-esteem**
- **Bullying**
- **Positive Behaviour Management**
- **Circle Time**
- **Anger Management**
- **Asperger's Syndrome**
- **Eating Disorders**

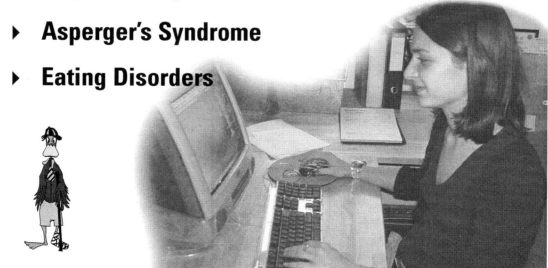

3 Thorndale Mews, Clifton, Bristol, BS8 2HX | Tel: +44 (0) 117 973 2881 Fax: +44 (0) 117 973 1707